Discover Your Path in Data

Data Analyst, Data Scientist, Data Engineer, Research Scientist, Business Operations & Strategy Analyst, Ops Analyst, Business Analyst. The data world has all of the above and many, many more roles. It doesn't matter if you're a college dropout or a PhD in computer science- with all of the options available, it can be incredibly difficult to understand what role you actually want.

This section has one intention: give you a comprehensive understanding of what role is right for you and what role you actually want. No matter how good you are, the interview process is an intense grind if you want to get something good, and without a true focus getting a great job may be impossible.

Kevin's Story

He felt ready. Kevin was brimming with confidence- he just finished a 3-month data course on Coursera in only 2 months. He struggled at times, but worked his tail off to learn the material and finish way ahead of schedule. All the early mornings, long nights, and full weekends of studying and grinding were finally about to pay off in the form of a fantastic new job in the tech industry. He'd been working as a marketing associate at a small financial services

com pany and was told, "Just focus on your job" when he asked about transitioning into an analyst role at the company. "They didn't think I could do it, but here I am," he thought. He was ready to reap the rewards of his hard work.

He started by taking a few hours to create a spreadsheet with potential jobs he'd apply for. He began his search on LinkedIn, and was impressed by how many role openings there were (and a little overwhelmed). He started adding them to the list: first lots of small companies, then adding some big fish like Google and Amazon. And why not? Sure, he didn't go to Stanford or Harvard, but he took the initiative and learned things on his own. Maybe that would be even better than going to a blue-chip college. Despite feeling a bit overwhelmed at first, Kevin got excited as he added more jobs to his spreadsheet- soon collecting over 30 roles that looked awesome: data science, data analytics, machine learning, even a few with "Engineer" in the title that looked really cool. He had so many skills that he felt is was just a matter of finding the right company and compensation, and he'd blow it out of the water.

Kevin read that he should apply to jobs Monday morning, so the application will be at the top of the recruiter's inbox. He set aside 30 minutes to polish his resume, then another 20 minutes to make sure he had the perfect mission statement at the top. He proofread the entire document word-for-word and looked loving at the final PDF, thinking, "I'm really doing it." Then, he dove right in- going through all the links, applying and even writing cover letters when possible to give it a special touch. After a few hours he double-checked the spreadsheet to make sure he'd applied to them all. The only thing left to do was wait.

So he waited. And waited. Nothing the first day. "No big deal," he thought, "It'd be crazy if they responded within a day." He focused on his day job for the rest of the day, and then went out to get beers with a few friends after work. When they asked him about the job hunt, he excitedly told them, "I'm pretty close. I'll probably be somewhere great within a month." The next day went by- nothing. "No big deal. Recruiters are super busy anyway." He took some time to review his notes and look up interview questions from some of his top companies.

Wednesday went by. He received two rejections that looked like automated responses. Attempting to rationalize, he thought, "Maybe those roles are already filled". He frantically checked his resume to see if he misspelled his email or something. He didn't. "It's fine. They get so many applicants, so it probably just takes some time," he thought.

Thursday: no response.

Friday: no response. He met up with some of the same friends he saw earlier in the week. "Hey Kevin, any interview lined up next week?" , they asked. "Um, no, not yet. Recruiters stay pretty busy so I don't have anything on the books yet, but I'm sure it will be soon." The weekend came and went without any updates. He figured that he wouldn't get any responses on Saturday or Sunday, but he did double-check his spam folder to be sure. Nothing in there. "Weird", he thought. Staying optimistic, he spent some time researching recruiter interview questions and even writing out his responses. He wanted to make sure he was 100% prepared for the calls he was sure he'd have the following week.

Monday: no response. Now, Kevin was getting stressed, and it showed. He had to deliver a report to his boss by end of day Monday, which he did, but his boss found a few simple math errors. This made him even more stressed, and the stress was starting to turn into frustration. Kevin clenched his teeth, "I do this report every month- how did I screw this up? How am I going to work in data if I can't even do this simple stuff right?"

The rest of the week dragged on as Kevin agonized over his inbox. Opening, refreshing, opening, refreshing. Nothing. One day he got a rejection letter, but just like before it was an automated response. He wondered if maybe something was wrong with the way his resume was formatted, or if recruiters weren't noticing the Coursera credential at the bottom, so he decided to reply to one of the rejection letters and politely ask if there was any feedback. This gave him a small boost of confidence because he figured he would just implement their ideas and be good to go. Unfortunately he discovered that wouldn't be possible: "Shoot, these are no-reply emails. I can't even ask a question."

Another week went by, leaving Kevin feeling dejected. Over 30 applications and not a single interview, not even a recruiter call. Knowing that persistence is key, he decided to spend the weekend collecting application links, and as he added roles he felt the excitement again. There were so many different roles at awesome companies that he felt he was bound to get something amazing. 20 links later he shut the laptop and decided to get some sleep- tomorrow he was going to hit the pavement and send out those applications.

He woke up early and got to work. First, he combed through his resume, examining every letter of every word of every line. It was immaculate. After a few adjustments to make his mission statement even more powerful, he gave the resume one more read-through and commenced the application process. He sped through the task, only doing cover letters for the biggest companies this time. He finished up in about an hour and started getting ready for his day job. "I've got it this time", he thought.

Monday went by. No response. Tuesday was the same. Around 10:30am on Wednesday a buzzing notification from his phone made him nearly jump out of his seat.

"Finally!" he thought as he read the email: "*We'd like to schedule you for a phone call to discuss the Sales Ops role*." This wasn't Google or anything, but it was an interesting-looking marketing technology company. He could use both his analytical skills and his marketing expertise (and maybe he'd get paid even more for having both). Kevin quickly emailed the recruiter with his availability and they scheduled the call.

He prepared. He wrote down all the questions he thought he might be asked, his answers, and even practiced saying them out loud. Kevin is no slouch. On the day of the interview he felt confident enough to climb a mountain or run through a wall.

The call began and they exchanged pleasantries quickly before getting down to business: "*Tell me about yourself*"

No problem- Kevin anticipated this question and gave a fantastic answer about his passion for analytics and how he spent most of his free time studying and learning the ropes. He could tell the recruiter was impressed.

"*What's your understanding of the Sales Ops role?*"

He wasn't planning on being asked this, but he took a moment to think and re-worded what he remembered from the job posting. Something about doing data deep dives, finding insights, and driving the strategy of the business. Not a perfect answer, but he felt it was OK. Besides, he had technical skills and let the recruiter know he's always open to learning more. The recruiter's response was a little less enthusiastic, but not bad or anything.

"*What's your experience working with sales teams?*"

"Not much" he replied, trying to make a joke. The recruiter didn't laugh, so he started talking again about his passion for data and how he's always open to learning more. Again he received a lukewarm response, but this time he just shrugged it off. "She's probably just tired. Recruiting is a very busy job," he thought.

"What kind of work interests you?"

Finally, one of the questions from his list. Kevin jumped right on it and started talking about how he thinks machine learning is so fascinating, and how he's spent a lot of time doing it and even did some small classification projects on his own. He even mentioned a few of his favorite models (Random Forest, Logistic Regression) and talked about why he likes decision trees but is always looking out for overfitting. "Awesome answer!" he thought to himself once he finished.

Silence on the line. "...OK. That sounds really cool.", the recruiter said, again not sounding very excited. Kevin reminded himself that she was probably just having a long day or doesn't want to show too much emotion on these calls.

At that point the recruiter wrapped up the interview and they said their goodbyes. Kevin made sure to thank her, and when he asked about next steps she simply said, "We'll email you and let you know". This was good enough for him. He met up with some friends that night and told them all about it.

"I have a good feeling about this one." he told them. In the moment he knew that he didn't have perfect answers, but that's to be expected. Nobody gives perfect answers, right? He had a little bit of nagging worry, but not much. Kevin knew he had to just focus on the next interview, which he figured would be with the hiring manager and would probably be more challenging.

The next morning his phone buzzed again, and Kevin opened his inbox excitedly.

"*Thank you for your application to ....*", **the subject line read.

He quickly opened the email to read the rest:

"*Thank you for applying to the Sales Operations Analyst role. We've had the privilege of talking to many great applicants, and at this time we're going to proceed with a candidate who's a stronger fit for the role.*"

Stunned, Kevin sat staring at the message. "Wow, really?", he thought. Kevin figured there would be some rejection, but you never quite feel it until it actually happens to you. "Oh well," he sighed, thinking about how his friends were going to ask for a status update. He wasn't looking forward to that conversation.

      The rest of the week went by without any responses (except a few rejection emails). The next week came and went in a similar fashion. That weekend he sat in his room and looked down at his progress tracker. One month, 50 applications, 1 interview. Lots of rejections. "What the heck is going on?", Kevin thought to himself. He decided to "get right back on the horse" and start applying to more jobs.

      What was Kevin's problem? Was his resume bad? Was he getting rejected because he didn't go to Stanford? Did people look down on marketers? No, no, no, and no.

      So what was it? Could it be that Kevin was getting rejected because he was just blasting out applications to whatever jobs looked "cool", rather than job that actually fit his skill set, experience, and interest? Let's dissect this idea.

Discover Your Path

In order to successfully make your next career move, you need to get clear on exactly what types of roles you're pursuing. You can still course-correct later and explore other options, but you need to have a specific outcome in mind if you want to actually get somewhere. Kevin didn't know what he actually wanted. He loved working with data and had the right skills, but he couldn't tell a Business Analyst from a Data Scientist from a Machine Learning Engineer.

Let's try a short exercise: Here are two actual answers people looking to begin a career in data gave to the same question: "What kind of role are you looking for?"

Person A: "I want to be a Data Scientist with a focus on analytics and the ability to apply fundamental statistical knowledge. My ideal role is one where I can flex my analytical chops and work cross-functionally to influence strategic business decisions"

Person B: "I want to work in data, and I'm really interested in doing data analysis in Python"

Which person do you think has a better chance of landing a job in data? By now, the answer should be obvious- Person A is going to understand which roles to go after and will have much more success interviewing with recruiters and hiring managers. Person B is going to struggle and may never get a job in data, let alone their ideal role.

So what does this mean for you? You probably have a basic idea of what data work interests you most, and this section is going to help you get incredibly clear on your vision and outline your specific, actionable outcome. With your outcome top-of-mind you'll increase your efficiency, need less study time, be able to speak to interviewers clearly and confidently, and most importantly- you'll dramatically increase your chance of landing your ideal role in data. Go through this section carefully and find your ideal path in data.

Let's get down to the nitty-gritty. There are a few things to think about when you're looking to start your career in data and need to choose the right path. Some examples:

- How much coding do you know? How much do you want to learn?
- Do you like probability and statistics? Are you willing to hit the books hard to get your stats knowledge up to par?
- What's your background? Is this your first technical role, or have you had other technical roles? Be honest here ("Marketing" is not a technical role). Remember that you can

still succeed if you don't have technical roles on your resume.
- Are you more of a strategy person who wants to work with non-technical audiences to drive business outcomes, or are you a "behind-the-scenes" expert who keeps everything running smoothly?

We'll take a full assessment at soon, but for now let these ideas marinate. It's important to know that to start out, you won't be able to do everything, and we also have to balance what is reasonable for you at this stage in your career. For example, Machine Learning is an incredibly interesting part of the data world, but if you've only got a year of experience in a non-technical role and don't know any coding languages, it will be extremely difficult to get an ML role.

Know this: if you're attempting to get your first role in data, just getting in is more important than getting your exact, ideal role. Once you have your foot in the door, you'll be able to hustle, prove yourself, learn from more senior people, and transition into bigger and better. You can get any role you want with the right strategy and work ethic- it just may take some time to get experience and build up your skills in a business setting.

Let's get started.

Data Path Assessment

For each question, circle or write down the letter in parentheses that corresponds to your preference. There may be questions where you like both choices- just go with your gut on which one you'd like more.

I prefer:

1. Setting up systems & processes (E) | Coming up with new ideas (A)

2. Database storage and technology (E) | Running experiments on user features (S)

3. Giving presentations to leaders in the company (A) | Using probability & statistics (S)

4. Working with non-technical people (A) | Working mostly with very technical people, such as software engineers (E)

5. Machine Learning (S) | Digging into problems and finding solutions (A)

6. Coding 100% of the time (E) | A mix of coding and non-coding (experiment analysis, communicating insights, etc) (S)

7. Running experiments (S) | Creating software infrastructure (E)

8. Supporting Non-Technical Teams (A) | Supporting Technical Teams (E)

9. Using Python (S) | Using a business intelligence tool such as Tableau (A)

10. Testing a Hypothesis (S) | Building a Data Pipeline (E)

11. Creating a data visualization (A) | Creating a new metric (S)

12. Maintaining a data warehouse (E) | Writing SQL (A)

Now, add up the number of times you circled A, S, and E. The letter with the highest score is the path that your preference align with the most:

A - Data Analyst
S - Data Scientist
E - Data Engineer

Let's get clear on a few things. First of all, all three career paths touch on all the topics mentioned above. Data Scientists use SQL, Data Analysts can be involved in running experiments, so on and so forth. This quiz is meant to give you a sense of what sort of roles you should look into as you're starting your job search.

Speaking of the job search, another important thing to mention is that data roles are highly depending on a given company's naming convention. Some companies have their Data Scientists work on Engineering problems. Some companies have Data Analysts work with lots of probability and statistics (typical Data Scientist skills). Some companies don't even have a, "Data Analyst" role, and instead call this group of employees Data Scientists.

Sound confusing? It certainly can be. All we want to do right now is to understand which way you're leaning, and then we'll dig into specific roles to figure out what roles specifically will be best for your interests and abilities. Let's begin the deep dive- here are the three buckets in more detail:

Analytics

Roles: Analyst, Business Analyst, Operations Analyst, Data Analyst, Data Scientist (Analytics Focus)

An analyst's main job is to have an in-depth understanding of the company's data stores, analyze that data, and look for patterns that can be assembled into insights. Analysts typically communicate insights and recommendations to company leaders in order to drive strategy. Some questions analysts might answer:

- Where should we invest in acquiring more customers?
- How often do our customers cancel, and what factors drive those cancellations?
- What's our go-to-market strategy for this new product?

There is an entire world of interesting work for an analyst to do at a company, particularly those in the technology space. Within the Analyst bucket there are many different roles with different responsibilities. That said, the core is the same: understand the data and use it to help drive the company forward.

Here are some of the roles in more detail:

Business Analyst: Business Analysts work closely with decision-makers to understand what the business needs and leverage data to help make decisions. For example, a business analyst may answer the question, "How do we cut waste and help our internal dashboarding tools work more efficiently?"

Operations Analyst: An Operations Analyst might do similar work as a Business Analyst. Someone in this role might be tasked with providing monthly reporting on various business processes and surfacing the most valuable insights to internal stakeholders.

Sales Operations Analyst: Sales Ops Analysts are almost always a role that supports the sales teams within a company. Some typical things this analyst may handle include pulling and packaging sales metrics, diagnosing the sales pipeline, and improving the team's productivity. If you have a background in sales, this is an excellent entry point into the world of data.

Marketing Analyst: Marketing Analysts understand marketing, but also have the technical skills to analyze the success or failure of marketing efforts. A typical day for a Marketing Analyst may include pulling lists for direct mail campaigns, analyzing email marketing campaigns, or working with a product marketing manager to test a new marketing idea. Those with a background in marketing and some technical skills often make great Marketing Analysts.

Revenue Analyst: This is an interesting role. Revenue Analysts are almost like accountants, but they get much deeper into the data and look for ways to increase revenue, as well as standard metrics reporting. This is a great move for someone who studied accounting or has worked in financial services before (and is interested in that kind of work).

Product Analyst: Product Analysts are often involved in some of the most interesting work at a company. These analysts are tasked with working on a specific product within a company (e.g. YouTube within Google), and they'll often do things like measuring usage, working with Product Managers to test new features, and evaluating product performance. If you've considered becoming a Product

Manager, or just have an interest in working on the product side of a company, this may be the role for you.

Data Analyst: If this role sounds broad, it's because it is. "Data Analyst" could mean any of the above roles or be essentially a Data Scientist, depending on the company. In general the tasks of a data analyst including digging through large amounts of data, finding insights, and communicating those insights to their team and leaders in the organization. SQL is a must, and often Data Analyst role postings love to see candidates with Python experience. The Data Analyst role is a great idea for someone who wants to work in more complex data topics (hard core statistics, machine learning), but may not be quite there yet in skill set or experience.

Data Scientist (Analytics Focus): What's a "Data Scientist" title doing in here? No, it's not a typo. Lately many companies have begun to rebrand their Data Analyst roles as "Data Scientist". The reason for this is they often need candidates to be fluent in Python, and in some cases want to see a foundational knowledge of statistics. This is a great role for someone with some experience in analytical roles who's put in the extra time to learn more challenging topics.

Data Scientist

Data Scientists are the brain-center of the organization, particularly in tech companies. They can serve a very wide variety of functions, but often their basic toolkit includes great analytical knowledge, above-average ability in probability and statistics, and, depending on the role, working knowledge of machine learning.

This is one of the most difficult career buckets to dissect because there is such a wide variety of actual job functions under the "Data Scientist" title. We will go more in depth, but the best way to help yourself understand which role is right for you, and which data scientist role is right for you, is to read job postings very carefully. In some industries or company segments, job postings may be more or less arbitrary- not true with Data Science! Data Scientist role postings almost always do a great job explaining accurately what the role responsibilities will be and what the requirements are.

Here's an example of a Data Scientist role posting:

Data Scientist at ABC Corp

- Master's degree or higher in Engineering, Math, Finance, Statistics, Computer Science, or other technical field from an accredited university.

- Experience processing, filtering, and presenting large quantities (Millions to Billions of rows) of data.

- Experience articulating business questions and using quantitative techniques to arrive at a solution using available data.

- 3+ years of hands on experience with statistical analysis, causal inferences, applying various machine learning techniques (e.g. ensembling, regularization, feature engineering), predictive modeling, and data mining.

- 3+ years of experience with data querying languages (e.g. SQL), scripting languages (e.g. Python), statistical/mathematical software (e.g. R, SAS, MATLAB), and machine learning packages (e.g. scikit-learn).

- Ability to develop experimental and analytic plans for data modeling processes, use of strong baselines, ability to accurately determine cause and effect relations.

- Demonstrable track record of dealing well with ambiguity, prioritizing needs, and delivering results in a dynamic environment.

- Excellent verbal and written communication skills with the ability to effectively advocate technical solutions to research scientists, engineering teams and business audiences.

And here's another example:

Data Scientist at XYZ, Inc:

- Professional industry experience in a quantitative analysis role (4+ years preferred).

- Comfortable in SQL and some experience with a programming language, with Python or R a plus.

- Ability to communicate clearly and effectively to cross functional partners of varying technical levels.

- Ability to define relevant metrics that can guide and influence stakeholders to the appropriate and accurate insights.

- Experience or willingness to learn tools to create data pipelines.

- Building clear and easy to understand dashboards (Tableau) and presentations.

Do they look the same? Not even close. This is why it is crucial to read job postings thoroughly when you're looking for roles. If you understand the job really well, you'll maximize your chances of actually getting an interview, and when you get an interview you'll do much better.

All of that said, before you start running to apply to Data Scientist roles, make sure that these general concepts appeal to you:

- Probability & statistics
- Experimentation
- Machine learning & modeling
- Working with non-technical stakeholders

If you find all of the above interesting, the Data Scientist path may be for you. It's probably a good idea to think about which of the above appeal to you most, and which of the above areas you're strongest in. By doing this you'll be able to recognize the right role immediately and not waste time applying to roles where you wouldn't be happy and successful.

There is one specific type of role worth mentioning here, within the Data Scientist path: Research Scientist. This is an interesting role that has existed in academia for a long time, but has recently come to prominence in private industry. Often these roles look very similar to Data Scientists, but the work tends to be even more focused on experimentation and heavy-duty machine learning algorithms. Research Scientists typically have PhDs- if you are interested in Data Science and come from a very scientific background/academia, this may be the path for you.

Data Engineer

If you're not as familiar with this role, you're not alone. Ironically this job doesn't usually make it to the "Sexiest Jobs of the 21st Century" list often, but Data Science and Analytics wouldn't even be possible without Data Engineers. These people often have a background in software engineering and are responsible for building and maintaining data pipelines and data stores.

If you've ever run a SQL query, a Data Engineer (or team of them) built that database. Doing anything with data would be impossible without a reliable infrastructure to extract, clean, store, and eventually retrieve crucial data. When a user hits the "Like" button, how does that click get counted? Ask a Data Engineer.

A few notes on this role: you'll likely have to have experience in serious coding and software engineering in order to move into one of these roles, and it will be hard to do if you're purely self-taught.

One path that many people take is to find a role that is more entry level (usually some sort of analyst), and then work their way into their ultimate, ideal role (data engineer or data scientist). This is a good idea for people who don't have a degree in a technical field or don't want to take on lots of additional education. This may actually benefit you in the long run since you'll be able to develop a very strong analytical foundation and then branch out into more challenging topics around software engineering and statistics.

Conclusion

What do you think? The last step in this section is to think about everything you've learned and decide what types of roles you're going to pursue. Keep in mind that you don't have to limit yourself to one segment forever- all we're doing is narrowing your focus initially so you'll be able to better connect with companies and increase your chances of getting a job offer for an exciting role.

Once you put yourself out there and refine your process, you'll learn more about the different roles and what might be best for you. This is an iterative process: you may start by pursuing Product Analyst roles, but then find that you're actually more interested in the sales side of analytics- then you can pursue a Sales Operations role.

Here's your formula:

1. Get clear on what the different segments are and what they mean: Data Analytics, Data Science, and Data Engineering.

2. Know yourself. Take the above assessment to find out which segment aligns with your interests and skills the most.

3. Dig deeper. Use the detailed breakdowns in this section to get a more thorough understanding of each segment and what different roles actually do.

4. Choose a path. Decide which path (and potentially which specific roles) you want to start pursuing. This will give you a specific focus and allow you to channel your

energy in one direction. Don't worry- you can always re-calibrate later.

Think you can handle this? Hopefully this is exciting for you. This is a crucial first step in your journey in the world of data careers. By understanding exactly what you want, you'll not only be able to focus your studies and connect with the right opportunities, but you'll also feel better about your decision and avoid making the wrong career move. Read through this section a few times and get clear on what path is right for you.

Thoughts from a Hiring Manager:
"One of the main things I look for in candidates is: are they actually interested in this job specifically? Do they really want to do the work that my team does, or are they just interested in the title/company/something else? You'd be surprised at the number of candidates who, when I ask them what kind of work they're looking to do, they respond with something that's totally different than the job description.

If the role doesn't mention machine learning and the interviewer doesn't ask about it, then don't bring up machine learning. Better yet, if machine learning is where you're really passionate, go get one of those roles (there's plenty). I don't need someone who's good at everything- I need someone who is great at a few relevant things and will be happy with the work not just a week after being hired, but 6 months and a year after being hired. I want people who join my team to be fulfilled and successful long-term."

www.ingramcontent.com/pod-product-compliance
Lightning Source LLC
Chambersburg PA
CBHW030558220526
45463CB00007B/3108